Chapter 1: Introduction to Self-Discovery and Empowerment 3

Understanding the Importance of Self-Discovery 3

Embracing Empowerment for Personal Growth 4

Chapter 2: Building Self-Awareness 6

Exploring Your Values and Beliefs 6

Identifying Your Strengths and Weaknesses 8

Recognizing Your Emotional Triggers 9

Cultivating Mindfulness and Present Moment Awareness 11

Chapter 3: Unleashing Your Inner Potential 13

Setting Meaningful Goals and Objectives 13

Developing a Growth Mindset 14

Overcoming Limiting Beliefs and Self-Doubt........................16

Harnessing the Power of Positive Thinking.........................17

Chapter 4: Nurturing Self-Compassion and Self-Love 19

Practicing Self-Care and Self-Nurturing 19

Embracing Imperfections and Practicing Forgiveness 21

Cultivating Gratitude and Appreciation................................22

Building Healthy Boundaries in Relationships......................24

Chapter 5: Exploring Your Passions and Purpose 25

Discovering Your Interests and Hobbies 25

Uncovering Your Core Values and Life Purpose....................27

Aligning Your Passions with Your Goals 29

Taking Action Towards Fulfillment 30

Chapter 6: Overcoming Obstacles and Adversity 32

Developing Resilience and Perseverance.............................32

Managing Stress and Anxiety..34

Coping with Failure and Rejection 35

Seeking Support and Building a Supportive Network 37

Chapter 7: Cultivating Healthy Relationships 38

Understanding the Importance of Healthy Relationships 38

Enhancing Communication Skills 40

Setting Boundaries and Respecting Others' Boundaries 42

Navigating Conflict and Resolving Issues 43

Chapter 8: Embracing Self-Expression and Authenticity 45

Discovering and Honoring Your True Self 45

Expressing Yourself Creatively 47

Embracing Your Unique Qualities and Individuality 48

Building Confidence and Assertiveness 50

Chapter 9: Igniting Personal Growth and Transformation 52

Continual Learning and Personal Development 52

Embracing Change and Adaptability 53

Taking Risks and Stepping Out of Your Comfort Zone 55

Celebrating Your Growth and Progress 56

Chapter 10: Sustaining Your True Self 58

Building Habits for Sustainable Self-Discovery 58

Creating a Supportive Environment 60

Practicing Self-Reflection and Evaluation 61

Embracing a Lifelong Journey of Self-Discovery 63

Conclusion: Embracing Your True Self and Empowering Others **64**

Chapter 1: Introduction to Self-Discovery and Empowerment

Understanding the Importance of Self-Discovery

In today's fast-paced world, it is easy to lose sight of who we truly are amidst the chaos and demands of daily life. In order to navigate through the challenges and uncertainties, it is crucial to embark on a journey of self-discovery. This subchapter aims to shed light on the importance of self-discovery and how it can empower both teens and adults to lead fulfilling lives.

Self-discovery is the process of understanding oneself on a deeper level – exploring our values, beliefs, passions, and purpose. It is a journey that allows us to uncover our true selves and make choices that align with our authentic desires, rather than conforming to societal expectations or external pressures.

One of the key benefits of self-discovery is enhanced self-awareness. By understanding our strengths, weaknesses, and triggers, we can make informed decisions and take control of our lives. This self-awareness acts as a compass, guiding us towards choices that bring us joy and fulfillment. Through self-reflection and introspection, we gain a clearer understanding of who we are and what truly matters to us.

Self-discovery also plays a vital role in personal growth and healing. By delving into our past experiences, traumas, and limiting beliefs, we can identify patterns that may be holding us back. This process allows us to let go of negative thoughts and emotions, and cultivate a positive mindset that supports our well-being. Through self-help techniques and practices, we can heal past wounds and develop resilience to overcome future challenges.

For teenagers, self-discovery is especially important as it helps them establish a strong sense of identity and purpose. By exploring their passions and interests, they can make informed decisions about their future education, career, and relationships. It empowers them to embrace their unique qualities and build self-confidence, enabling them to navigate the complexities of adolescence with resilience and authenticity.

In conclusion, self-discovery is a transformative journey that holds great significance in the realm of self-help. It allows individuals to uncover their true selves, enhance self-awareness, and cultivate personal growth and healing. By understanding who we are at our core, we can make choices that align with our values and lead fulfilling lives. Whether you are a teen or an adult, embarking on the path of self-discovery is a powerful step towards unlocking your true self and living a life of empowerment.

Embracing Empowerment for Personal Growth

Empowerment is a transformative journey that allows individuals to tap into their inner strength, realize their potential, and take charge of their lives. In this subchapter, we will explore the concept of empowerment and how it can contribute to personal growth, specifically targeting teens and adults seeking self-help and guidance.

To truly unlock your true self and embark on a path of self-discovery, it is crucial to embrace empowerment. Empowerment is about recognizing your worth, building self-confidence, and taking control of your choices and actions. It is a process that requires self-reflection, awareness, and a commitment to personal growth.

One of the key aspects of embracing empowerment is self-reflection. This involves taking the time to understand your strengths, weaknesses, desires, and values. By asking yourself the right questions, such as "What are my passions? What are my fears?

What are my goals?", you begin to gain a deeper understanding of who you are and what you want to achieve. This self-reflection lays the foundation for personal growth.

Awareness is another vital component of empowerment. It involves being conscious of your thoughts, emotions, and behaviors. By cultivating self-awareness, you can identify negative patterns, limiting beliefs, and self-imposed barriers that hinder your progress. This newfound awareness allows you to make conscious choices and take responsibility for your actions, leading to personal growth and positive change.

In the journey of self-help, empowerment serves as a catalyst for healing and anti-anxiety. By embracing empowerment, you can overcome self-doubt, anxiety, and insecurities that may be holding you back. It enables you to develop resilience, cope with challenges, and build a strong foundation for mental well-being.

Empowerment is not a destination but a lifelong process. It requires consistent effort, self-care, and a commitment to personal growth. By embracing empowerment, you can unlock your true potential, cultivate self-confidence, and create a fulfilling life aligned with your values and aspirations.

In this subchapter, we will provide you with 300 questions for self-reflection, awareness, discovery, healing, and anti-anxiety. These questions will guide you on your journey of self-help and empowerment, helping you unlock your true self, embrace personal growth, and find inner peace and fulfillment.

Remember, empowerment starts from within. By embracing it, you take the first step towards unlocking your true self and living a life of purpose, joy, and authenticity.

Chapter 2: Building Self-Awareness

Exploring Your Values and Beliefs

In the journey of self-discovery and empowerment, understanding your values and beliefs is a crucial step towards unlocking your true self. Your values and beliefs shape your identity, guide your decisions, and influence your actions. By delving into this subchapter, you will embark on a transformative exploration of your innermost principles and convictions.

Values serve as the compass that directs your life's path. They are the fundamental principles that define what is important to you, what you stand for, and what you strive to achieve. Reflecting on your values will help you gain clarity about your priorities, enabling you to align your actions with what truly matters to you.

To begin this journey, ask yourself thought-provoking questions such as: What do I value most in life? What principles guide my decisions? What traits do I admire in others? By contemplating these questions, you will gain insights into the values that shape your character.

Beliefs, on the other hand, are the ideas and convictions you hold about yourself, others, and the world around you. They are the lenses through which you perceive and interpret reality. Exploring your beliefs will allow you to uncover any limiting or empowering ideas that influence your thoughts, emotions, and behaviors.

Challenge your beliefs by asking yourself: Are my beliefs based on evidence or assumptions? Are they helping or hindering my growth? Are there any alternative perspectives that I should consider? By critically examining your beliefs, you can let go of those that no longer serve you and adopt new empowering ones that align with your aspirations.

As you explore your values and beliefs, it is essential to approach this process with curiosity, open-mindedness, and self-compassion. Remember that your values and beliefs may evolve over time as you gain new experiences and knowledge. Embrace this growth and allow yourself the freedom to adapt and change along your journey.

Ultimately, understanding your values and beliefs empowers you to live a more authentic and purpose-driven life. It helps you make decisions that resonate with your true self, build meaningful relationships, and pursue goals that align with your core values. By exploring this aspect of yourself, you lay the foundation for personal growth, self-acceptance, and fulfillment.

Unlocking Your True Self: A Teen's Guide to Self-Discovery and Empowerment offers you a treasure trove of 300 questions for self-reflection, awareness, discovery, healing, and anti-anxiety. Within this book's pages, you will find the tools to navigate the vast landscape of self-help, supporting both teens and adults in their journey towards self-discovery and personal transformation. So, dive into the subchapter on exploring your values and beliefs and unlock the keys to your true self.

Identifying Your Strengths and Weaknesses

Understanding our strengths and weaknesses is a crucial step towards self-discovery and personal empowerment. By recognizing and harnessing our strengths, we can build confidence, pursue our goals, and create a fulfilling life. Similarly, acknowledging our weaknesses allows us to identify areas for improvement and develop strategies to overcome obstacles. In this chapter, we will explore the process of identifying our strengths and weaknesses, and how this knowledge can positively impact our lives.

The first step in this journey is self-reflection. Take the time to ask yourself important questions such as: What am I good at? What activities make me feel energized and fulfilled? What are my passions and interests? By diving deep into these questions, you will begin to uncover your unique strengths and talents. Remember, everyone has their own set of strengths, and it's important not to compare yourself to others. Focus on what makes you special and embrace it.

Next, it's time to examine your weaknesses. These are areas where you may struggle or need improvement. Be honest with yourself and identify where you may face challenges. This is not meant to discourage you, but rather to help you grow. Recognizing your weaknesses allows you to seek support, learn new skills, or develop strategies to overcome obstacles. Remember, weaknesses are not permanent limitations; they are opportunities for growth and development.

Once you have a clear understanding of your strengths and weaknesses, it's important to leverage them effectively. Use your strengths to your advantage, whether it's in pursuing your passions, choosing a career path, or building relationships. By focusing on your strengths, you can cultivate confidence and achieve success in areas that align with your natural abilities.

On the other hand, don't shy away from your weaknesses. Instead, view them as areas for growth and improvement. Seek out resources, mentors, or educational opportunities that can help you overcome these challenges. Remember, growth comes from stepping outside of your comfort zone and embracing new experiences.

In conclusion, identifying your strengths and weaknesses is a vital step in self-discovery and personal empowerment. Embrace your strengths, leverage them to your advantage, and pursue your passions. At the same time, acknowledge your weaknesses, seek growth opportunities, and never be afraid to ask for help. By understanding and embracing your true self, you have the power to unlock your full potential and create a fulfilling life.

Recognizing Your Emotional Triggers

In our journey of self-discovery and empowerment, it is crucial to recognize and understand our emotional triggers. These triggers are the events, situations, or thoughts that can cause intense emotional reactions within us. They have the power to set off a cascade of emotions, often leading to anxiety, stress, or even harmful behaviors. By identifying and understanding our triggers, we can develop healthier coping mechanisms and take charge of our emotional well-being.

Recognizing emotional triggers requires self-reflection and awareness. It involves paying close attention to our thoughts, feelings, and behaviors during moments of heightened emotions. By doing so, we can start noticing patterns and identifying the specific triggers that cause us distress. These triggers can vary from person to person, as we all have unique experiences and sensitivities.

One way to recognize your emotional triggers is to keep a journal. Write down the situations or events that evoke strong emotions within you. Reflect on how you felt, what thoughts crossed your mind, and how you reacted. Over time, you may notice recurring themes or patterns that can help you better understand your triggers.

Another effective method is mindfulness meditation. By practicing mindfulness, we learn to observe our thoughts and emotions without judgment. When an emotional trigger arises, instead of reacting impulsively, we can take a step back and observe our reactions. This allows us to gain insight into the underlying causes of our emotional reactions.

Recognizing emotional triggers also involves examining our past experiences and traumas. Sometimes, our triggers can be deeply rooted in past events that have left a lasting impact on our emotional well-being. By seeking therapy or counseling, we can explore these experiences in a safe and supportive environment, allowing us to heal and gain a better understanding of our triggers.

Once we have identified our emotional triggers, it becomes easier to develop strategies to manage them. This may involve practicing self-care techniques such as deep breathing exercises, engaging in hobbies or activities that bring us joy, or seeking support from loved ones. By taking proactive steps to address our triggers, we can regain control over our emotions and foster a greater sense of self-empowerment.

Recognizing your emotional triggers is an essential part of self-help and personal growth. It allows us to gain a deeper understanding of ourselves, develop healthier coping mechanisms, and ultimately unlock our true selves. By embarking on this journey, you are taking a significant step towards self-discovery, healing, and anti-anxiety. Remember, you have the power to shape your emotional well-being and lead a more fulfilling life.

Cultivating Mindfulness and Present Moment Awareness

In today's fast-paced world, it can be challenging to stay centered and fully present in the moment. However, cultivating mindfulness and present moment awareness is a powerful tool for self-discovery, healing, and empowerment. This subchapter explores various techniques and practices to help you unlock your true self through the practice of mindfulness.

Mindfulness is the practice of intentionally paying attention to the present moment without judgment. It involves bringing your awareness to your thoughts, feelings, bodily sensations, and the environment around you. By practicing mindfulness, you can learn to observe your thoughts and emotions without getting caught up in them, thus gaining a sense of clarity and calmness.

One effective way to cultivate mindfulness is through meditation. Meditation is a practice that involves focusing your attention and eliminating the stream of thoughts that often overwhelms your mind.

By dedicating just a few minutes each day to meditation, you can train your mind to be more present and aware, reducing stress and anxiety in the process.

Another technique to enhance mindfulness is practicing gratitude. Gratitude involves acknowledging and appreciating the positive aspects of your life. By consciously focusing on what you are grateful for, you shift your attention away from negative thoughts and cultivate a more positive mindset, fostering self-discovery and empowerment.

Additionally, incorporating mindful eating into your daily routine can help you develop a deeper connection with your body and the food you consume. Paying attention to the taste, texture, and sensations while eating can enhance your awareness and appreciation of nourishing your body, leading to a healthier relationship with food and self.

Furthermore, engaging in mindful movement practices such as yoga or tai chi can help you connect with your body and breath. These practices promote physical and mental well-being, allowing you to become more grounded and centered in the present moment.

By cultivating mindfulness and present moment awareness, you can unlock your true self and empower yourself to navigate life's challenges with grace and resilience. Through the practices of meditation, gratitude, mindful eating, and mindful movement, you can develop a deeper understanding of yourself, heal emotional wounds, and reduce anxiety. Embracing these techniques will enable you to live a more fulfilling and authentic life, enhancing your overall well-being and self-discovery journey.

In conclusion, cultivating mindfulness and present moment awareness is a powerful tool for self-help and self-discovery. By incorporating practices such as meditation, gratitude, mindful eating, and mindful movement into your daily life, you can unlock your true self and empower yourself to live a more authentic and fulfilling life.

So, take a moment, breathe, and embark on this transformative journey towards self-awareness and healing.

Chapter 3: Unleashing Your Inner Potential

Setting Meaningful Goals and Objectives

In the journey of self-discovery and empowerment, setting meaningful goals and objectives plays a pivotal role. It provides a roadmap to navigate through life's challenges and helps individuals align their actions with their true selves. Whether you are a teen or an adult seeking self-help, understanding the importance of setting meaningful goals can bring about positive changes in your life.

To begin with, setting goals gives your life direction and purpose. It allows you to envision the kind of person you want to become and the life you wish to lead. Without clear goals, you may find yourself drifting aimlessly, lacking motivation and focus. By setting meaningful goals, you give yourself something to strive for, igniting a sense of passion and determination.

Moreover, setting goals helps you prioritize your actions and make better decisions. When you have a clear objective in mind, you can evaluate your choices based on whether they align with your goals or not. This helps you avoid distractions and focus on what truly matters. It also enables you to develop a sense of discipline and self-control, as you work towards achieving your objectives.

Furthermore, setting goals allows for personal growth and development. By setting challenging yet attainable goals, you push yourself to step out of your comfort zone and expand your horizons. This leads to self-improvement, as you acquire new skills, knowledge, and experiences along the way. With each goal accomplished, you gain confidence and a sense of accomplishment, fueling your motivation to tackle even greater challenges.

However, it is important to set meaningful goals that resonate with your values and aspirations. Reflect on your true self and identify what truly matters to you. Consider your passions, interests, and long-term vision. Your goals should be in alignment with your authenticity, as this will bring about a deeper sense of fulfillment and satisfaction.

In conclusion, setting meaningful goals and objectives is an essential aspect of self-discovery and empowerment. It provides direction, focus, and purpose to your life, helping you make informed decisions and prioritize your actions. Through setting goals, you can experience personal growth and development, as you challenge yourself to step out of your comfort zone. Remember to align your goals with your true self, ensuring they reflect your values and aspirations. Embrace the power of goal-setting and unlock your true potential.

Developing a Growth Mindset

In today's fast-paced and ever-changing world, the ability to adapt and grow is crucial for personal development and success. This subchapter focuses on developing a growth mindset, a powerful tool that can help individuals navigate through challenges, overcome obstacles, and unlock their true potential.

A growth mindset is the belief that one's abilities and intelligence can be developed through dedication and hard work. It is the understanding that failure is not a setback, but an opportunity to learn and grow. By cultivating a growth mindset, individuals can improve their skills, increase their resilience, and foster a positive outlook on life.

To develop a growth mindset, it is essential to start by embracing challenges. Instead of shying away from difficult tasks, view them as opportunities for growth. Take on new challenges, push yourself out of your comfort zone, and be willing to make mistakes. Remember, each mistake is a chance to learn and improve.

Another important aspect of developing a growth mindset is to cultivate a sense of perseverance. Understand that success does not come overnight and that setbacks are a natural part of the journey. Stay determined, committed, and resilient, even when faced with obstacles. Believe in your ability to overcome challenges and keep moving forward.

Effort and hard work play a vital role in developing a growth mindset. Understand that talent alone is not enough to achieve success. Dedicate yourself to continuous learning, practice, and improvement. Embrace a mindset of constant growth and remain open to new knowledge and experiences.

In addition to effort, seeking feedback and learning from others is crucial in developing a growth mindset. Surround yourself with mentors, coaches, and supportive individuals who can provide constructive criticism and guidance. Use feedback as an opportunity to learn and grow, and be open to different perspectives.

Finally, developing a growth mindset requires cultivating a positive attitude towards failure. Instead of viewing failure as a reflection of your abilities, see it as a stepping stone towards success. Learn from each failure, adjust your approach, and keep moving forward with renewed determination.

By developing a growth mindset, individuals can unlock their true potential and achieve personal growth and success. Embrace challenges, persevere through obstacles, put in the effort, seek feedback, and reframe failure. With a growth mindset, the possibilities for self-discovery and empowerment are endless.

Overcoming Limiting Beliefs and Self-Doubt

In our journey of self-discovery and empowerment, one of the biggest obstacles we face is our own limiting beliefs and self-doubt. These internal barriers can hold us back from reaching our true potential and living a fulfilling life. However, with the right mindset and strategies, we can break free from these shackles and unlock our true selves.

The first step in overcoming limiting beliefs is to identify them. Take a moment to reflect on your thoughts and beliefs about yourself and your abilities. Are there any recurring negative thoughts or self-defeating beliefs that hold you back? Write them down and examine them closely. By recognizing these limiting beliefs, you can begin to challenge and replace them with more empowering ones.

Next, it's important to understand where these beliefs come from. Often, they stem from past experiences, societal expectations, or comparisons to others. It's essential to realize that these beliefs are not facts but rather interpretations we have formed over time. By questioning their validity and recognizing that they are not serving us, we can start to let go of them.

To overcome self-doubt, it's crucial to build self-confidence. Start by acknowledging your strengths and accomplishments. Make a list of all the things you are proud of and remind yourself of them regularly. Surround yourself with positive influences and supportive people who believe in you and your abilities. By cultivating a positive environment, you can boost your self-esteem and combat self-doubt.

Another powerful tool in overcoming limiting beliefs and self-doubt is affirmations. Affirmations are positive statements that you repeat to yourself daily. They help reprogram your subconscious mind and replace negative thoughts with empowering ones. Choose affirmations that resonate with you and repeat them aloud or write them down regularly. With consistent practice, you will start to believe in yourself and your abilities more deeply.

Remember, overcoming limiting beliefs and self-doubt is a journey, and it requires patience and perseverance. Be kind to yourself and celebrate small victories along the way. Embrace the process of self-discovery and continue to challenge and grow beyond your perceived limitations. As you do, you will unlock your true self and live a life of empowerment and fulfillment.

Harnessing the Power of Positive Thinking

In a world filled with constant challenges and uncertainties, it is crucial for individuals to cultivate a positive mindset. The power of positive thinking can truly transform one's life, providing a strong foundation for self-discovery, empowerment, and personal growth. In this subchapter, we will explore the significance of harnessing the power of positive thinking and how it can benefit both teens and adults in their journey of self-help and self-improvement.

Positive thinking is not just about wishful thinking or ignoring the harsh realities of life. Rather, it is a mindset that enables individuals to approach situations with optimism, resilience, and a belief in their ability to overcome obstacles. By adopting a positive mindset, individuals can reframe their thoughts, focusing on possibilities instead of limitations, and finding solutions instead of dwelling on problems.

The benefits of positive thinking are numerous and far-reaching. It can enhance overall mental well-being, reduce stress, anxiety, and depression, and improve physical health. Positive thinking also plays a vital role in building self-confidence, motivation, and resilience, allowing individuals to face challenges head-on and bounce back from setbacks.

For teenagers, in particular, harnessing the power of positive thinking is essential for self-discovery and empowerment. Adolescence is a period of immense change, both physically and emotionally, and it can be overwhelming at times. By cultivating a positive mindset, teenagers can navigate through this transformative phase with confidence and self-assurance.

Adults, too, can greatly benefit from the power of positive thinking. Whether they are facing career challenges, relationship issues, or personal struggles, maintaining a positive mindset can help them navigate through these difficulties. It provides a sense of control, enabling adults to make better decisions and take actions that align with their goals and values.

To harness the power of positive thinking, individuals can incorporate various practices into their daily lives. These may include affirmations, gratitude exercises, visualization techniques, and surrounding oneself with positive influences and supportive individuals. Additionally, practicing self-care, engaging in hobbies, and setting realistic goals can also contribute to maintaining a positive mindset.

In conclusion, harnessing the power of positive thinking is a crucial aspect of self-help and self-improvement for both teenagers and adults. By adopting a positive mindset, individuals can unlock their true potential, embrace self-discovery, and empower themselves to overcome challenges. Through the cultivation of positive thinking, one can embark on a transformative journey towards personal growth, healing, and a more fulfilling life.

Chapter 4: Nurturing Self-Compassion and Self-Love

Practicing Self-Care and Self-Nurturing

In today's fast-paced and demanding world, it is easy to neglect our own needs and focus solely on external responsibilities and expectations. However, taking care of ourselves is essential for our well-being and overall happiness. In this subchapter, we will explore the importance of self-care and self-nurturing, providing you with practical tips and strategies to incorporate these practices into your daily life.

Self-care encompasses various activities and habits that promote physical, emotional, and mental well-being. It is about prioritizing yourself and ensuring that you are meeting your own needs. This can include engaging in activities that bring you joy and relaxation, setting boundaries to protect your energy and time, and developing healthy habits such as exercise, eating well, and getting enough sleep.

While self-care is often associated with indulgence or selfishness, it is actually an act of self-compassion and self-love. By taking care of yourself, you are better equipped to take care of others and navigate life's challenges. Self-nurturing, on the other hand, involves providing yourself with the emotional support and encouragement necessary for personal growth and development.

One important aspect of self-care and self-nurturing is self-reflection. By taking the time to understand your own needs, values, and desires, you can make conscious choices that align with your authentic self. Journaling, mindfulness practices, and engaging in creative activities can help you access your inner thoughts and emotions, fostering self-awareness and self-discovery.

Additionally, practicing self-care and self-nurturing can be a powerful tool for managing anxiety and promoting healing. By engaging in activities that promote relaxation and stress relief, such as meditation, deep breathing exercises, or engaging in hobbies you enjoy, you can reduce anxiety and improve your overall mental health.

Remember, self-help and self-care are ongoing processes that require commitment and practice. It is important to be patient and kind to yourself as you navigate this journey of self-discovery and empowerment. By incorporating self-care and self-nurturing into your daily life, you can unlock your true self and cultivate a greater sense of well-being and fulfillment.

In conclusion, prioritizing self-care and self-nurturing is crucial for personal growth and overall well-being. By incorporating these practices into your life, you can enhance your self-awareness, manage anxiety, and foster a greater sense of self-empowerment. Remember, you deserve to take care of yourself, and by doing so, you can unlock your true self and live a more fulfilling and joyful life.

Embracing Imperfections and Practicing Forgiveness

In the journey of self-discovery and empowerment, it is crucial to understand and embrace the concept of imperfections and forgiveness. These two fundamental aspects of personal growth go hand in hand, helping us navigate through life's challenges and empowering us to unlock our true selves.

Imperfections are an inherent part of being human. Each one of us has flaws, makes mistakes, and falls short in certain areas of our lives. However, it is essential to recognize that these imperfections do not define us. They are simply opportunities for growth and learning. By embracing our imperfections, we open ourselves up to self-acceptance and self-compassion.

Often, we tend to be our harshest critics, constantly striving for perfection. But in reality, perfection is an illusion. It is an unattainable standard that only leads to frustration and self-doubt. Instead, we should focus on progress and personal growth. Embracing our imperfections allows us to let go of unrealistic expectations and embrace ourselves as we are, flaws and all.

Practicing forgiveness is another crucial aspect of self-help and personal development. Holding onto grudges, resentment, or anger only weighs us down, hindering our ability to move forward. Forgiveness is not about condoning the actions of others, but rather freeing ourselves from the burden of negativity. It is a gift we give ourselves, allowing us to find peace and move forward with our lives.

Forgiveness is a process that requires patience and self-reflection. It involves acknowledging our own pain and hurt, understanding the perspective of the other person, and ultimately choosing to let go and release the negative emotions associated with the situation. It is a powerful act of self-empowerment and a step towards personal healing.

By embracing our imperfections and practicing forgiveness, we create space for personal growth, self-compassion, and emotional well-being. It is through these practices that we unlock our true selves and discover our inner strength and resilience.

In conclusion, embracing imperfections and practicing forgiveness are vital components of self-help and personal development. By acknowledging our imperfections and letting go of grudges, we create a pathway to self-acceptance, personal growth, and emotional healing. So, let us embrace our imperfections, forgive ourselves and others, and unlock our true selves on this journey of self-discovery and empowerment.

Cultivating Gratitude and Appreciation

In today's fast-paced world, it's easy to get caught up in the hustle and bustle of everyday life. We often find ourselves focusing on the things we don't have or the challenges we face, rather than appreciating the blessings and opportunities that surround us. However, cultivating gratitude and appreciation can have a transformative effect on our lives, helping us find joy and contentment in even the smallest of things.

Gratitude is the practice of recognizing and acknowledging the good in our lives, while appreciation involves expressing gratitude and showing kindness towards others. Both gratitude and appreciation are powerful tools that can help us shift our perspective, increase our happiness, and improve our overall well-being.

In this subchapter, we will explore the importance of cultivating gratitude and appreciation in our daily lives. We will learn practical strategies and exercises to help us develop this mindset and make it a part of our daily routine. By doing so, we can unlock our true selves and experience a greater sense of self-discovery and empowerment.

One of the first steps in cultivating gratitude and appreciation is to start a gratitude journal. This simple practice involves writing down three things we are grateful for each day. By focusing on the positive aspects of our lives, we train our minds to seek out and appreciate the good, even in challenging situations.

Another powerful exercise is the "gratitude letter." This involves writing a heartfelt letter to someone we appreciate and expressing our gratitude for their presence in our lives. This not only strengthens our relationships but also helps us recognize the impact others have on our well-being.

In addition to these exercises, we will explore the benefits of practicing mindfulness and meditation. These practices help us become more present and aware, allowing us to fully appreciate the beauty and abundance that surrounds us.

By cultivating gratitude and appreciation, we can create a positive shift in our lives. We can develop a greater sense of self-awareness, improve our relationships, and increase our overall happiness. So, let's embark on this journey together and unlock our true selves through the power of gratitude and appreciation.

Building Healthy Boundaries in Relationships

In the journey of self-discovery and empowerment, one crucial aspect that often gets overlooked is the importance of building healthy boundaries in relationships. Whether it's with friends, family, or romantic partners, establishing and maintaining strong boundaries is essential for your overall well-being and personal growth.

Boundaries define the limits of what is acceptable to you in a relationship. They help you establish your own identity and protect your emotional, mental, and physical space. Without healthy boundaries, you may find yourself feeling overwhelmed, taken advantage of, or constantly sacrificing your own needs and desires for others.

To begin building healthy boundaries, it's important to first identify your values, beliefs, and personal limits. Reflect on what makes you comfortable or uncomfortable in different situations. Ask yourself questions like: What are my non-negotiables in a relationship? How do I want to be treated? What are my deal-breakers?

Once you have a clear understanding of your boundaries, it's essential to communicate them effectively. This means expressing your needs, desires, and limits to others in a respectful and assertive manner. Remember, setting boundaries is not about controlling or manipulating others; it's about taking care of yourself and ensuring your well-being.

Be prepared for some resistance or pushback when you start asserting your boundaries. Some people may not be used to you standing up for yourself, but it's important to stay firm and consistent. Surround yourself with individuals who respect and honor your boundaries, and be willing to let go of toxic relationships that continuously disregard them.

Maintaining healthy boundaries also requires self-awareness and self-care. Regularly check in with yourself to see if your boundaries are being respected and if any adjustments need to be made. Practice self-compassion and give yourself permission to say no when something doesn't align with your values or feels overwhelming.

Building healthy boundaries in relationships is an ongoing process. It takes time, practice, and self-reflection to establish and maintain them effectively. However, the rewards are immense. By setting and enforcing your boundaries, you create a space for authentic connections, mutual respect, and personal growth.

Remember, you have the power to define your own boundaries and shape the dynamics of your relationships. Embrace this power, honor your needs, and unlock the true potential of your relationships by building healthy boundaries.

Chapter 5: Exploring Your Passions and Purpose

Discovering Your Interests and Hobbies

In this subchapter, we will explore the wonderful world of interests and hobbies. Whether you are a teenager or an adult, it is essential to discover and pursue activities that bring you joy and fulfillment. This chapter will guide you through the process of identifying your interests and hobbies, and help you understand how they can contribute to your self-discovery and empowerment.

1. The Importance of Interests and Hobbies, Interests and hobbies are not just a way to pass the time; they are an integral part of who you are. Your interests reflect your passions, values, and personality. Engaging in activities you truly enjoy can enhance your overall well-being, boost self-confidence, and provide a sense of purpose.

2. Self-Reflection and Awareness, To discover your interests and hobbies, it is crucial to engage in self-reflection and self-awareness. Ask yourself questions like: What activities make me lose track of time? What subjects or topics do I find myself constantly researching? What activities make me feel alive and energized?

Reflecting on these questions will help you uncover your true passions.

3. Exploring Different Activities, Don't be afraid to try new things! The journey to discovering your interests and hobbies involves exploring various activities. Attend workshops, join clubs, volunteer, or simply experiment with different hobbies. Every experience will contribute to your self-discovery and broaden your horizons.

4. Embracing Your Unique Hobbies, Remember, there are no right or wrong hobbies. Each person has unique interests that make them who they are. Embrace your individuality and pursue hobbies that genuinely resonate with you, regardless of societal expectations or trends. Your hobbies should reflect your true self, not someone else's expectations.

5. The Power of Passion Projects, Once you have identified your interests and hobbies, consider turning them into passion projects. Passion projects are activities that you are deeply passionate about and can dedicate your time and energy to. They can provide a sense of purpose and fulfillment, and may even lead to future career opportunities.

Conclusion: Discovering your interests and hobbies is a transformative journey that contributes to your self-discovery and empowerment. By engaging in self-reflection, exploring various activities, and embracing your unique passions, you can unlock a world of joy, fulfillment, and personal growth. Remember, your hobbies are not just activities; they are an integral part of your true self. So, dive into the adventure of self-discovery and unlock the limitless possibilities that lie within your interests and hobbies.

Uncovering Your Core Values and Life Purpose

In our journey towards self-discovery and empowerment, understanding our core values and life purpose is crucial. These foundational elements shape who we are, what we believe in, and guide us towards a fulfilling and meaningful life. By delving deep into these aspects of ourselves, we gain clarity, direction, and a sense of purpose.

Core values are the fundamental beliefs and principles that define our character and guide our actions. They are the compass that helps us make decisions, set goals, and prioritize our lives. Identifying our core values requires introspection and self-reflection. Ask yourself, what principles do I hold dear? What qualities do I admire in others? What motivates and inspires me? By answering these questions, we can uncover our core values and align our lives with them.

Once we have a clear understanding of our core values, the next step is to discover our life purpose. Our purpose is the reason why we exist, the unique contributions we can make to the world. It is the driving force behind our actions and the source of our fulfillment. Discovering our life purpose involves exploring our passions, talents, and the impact we want to create. Reflect on what activities bring you joy and fulfillment. What are your natural talents and skills? How can you use them to make a difference in the lives of others?

Uncovering our core values and life purpose is a continuous process. As we grow and evolve, these aspects of ourselves might shift and change. It is essential to regularly reassess and realign ourselves with our core values and life purpose to ensure we are living authentically and in alignment with our true selves.

By understanding our core values and life purpose, we gain a sense of clarity and direction. We can make decisions that are in line with our values and pursue paths that bring us closer to our life purpose. This self-awareness empowers us to live a life that is authentic and fulfilling.

In conclusion, uncovering our core values and life purpose is a vital step in our journey towards self-discovery and empowerment. By delving deep into these aspects of ourselves, we gain clarity, direction, and a sense of purpose. Take the time to reflect on your core values and explore your passions and talents to discover your unique life purpose. By aligning your actions with your values and purpose, you can live a life that is authentic, meaningful, and fulfilling.

Aligning Your Passions with Your Goals

In the journey of self-discovery and empowerment, it is crucial to align your passions with your goals. This subchapter will delve into the importance of recognizing your passions and how they can fuel your journey towards achieving your goals. By understanding this vital connection, you can unlock your true self and live a fulfilling and purpose-driven life.

Passions are the driving force behind our actions and aspirations. They are the things that ignite a fire within us and bring us immense joy and fulfillment. Whether it's art, sports, music, writing, or any other pursuit, our passions have the power to shape our lives in profound ways.

When we align our passions with our goals, we tap into an incredible source of motivation and inspiration. When our goals are driven by our passions, they become more meaningful and purposeful. Rather than merely chasing external validation or societal expectations, we strive for something that truly resonates with our authentic selves.

Identifying your passions is the first step towards aligning them with your goals. Take some time for self-reflection and ask yourself what activities bring you the most joy and fulfillment. What makes you lose track of time? What are the things you could do endlessly without feeling tired or bored? These are likely your passions, and they hold the key to unlocking your true self.

Once you've identified your passions, it's important to set goals that align with them. Your goals should reflect your passions and provide a roadmap for pursuing them. For example, if your passion lies in art, your goals might include attending an art school, showcasing your work in galleries, or even starting your own art business.

Aligning your passions with your goals also requires a deep understanding of yourself. It involves recognizing your strengths, weaknesses, values, and beliefs. By understanding yourself on a deeper level, you can ensure that your goals are in line with your true self, rather than being influenced by external factors or societal pressures.

It's important to note that aligning your passions with your goals is not a one-time process. As you grow and evolve, your passions may change, and your goals will need to be adjusted accordingly. Embrace this fluidity and be open to exploring new passions and setting new goals as you progress on your journey of self-discovery.

In conclusion, aligning your passions with your goals is the key to unlocking your true self and living a purposeful life. By recognizing your passions, setting goals that reflect them, and understanding yourself on a deeper level, you can embark on a journey of self-discovery and empowerment. Embrace your passions, chase your dreams, and let them guide you towards a life filled with fulfillment and happiness.

Taking Action Towards Fulfillment

In the journey of self-discovery and empowerment, it is crucial to take action towards fulfillment. The process of unlocking your true self requires active participation and a willingness to make positive changes in your life. In this subchapter, we will explore various aspects of taking action and how it can lead to a more fulfilling life.

One of the first steps towards fulfillment is setting goals. By identifying what you want to achieve, you create a roadmap for your journey. Start by asking yourself questions like: What are my passions? What brings me joy? What do I want to accomplish in the short-term and long-term? These questions will help you gain clarity and define your aspirations.

Once you have set your goals, it is important to break them down into smaller, manageable steps. This approach makes them less overwhelming and enables you to take consistent action. Each small step you take brings you closer to your desired outcome, giving you a sense of progress and accomplishment.

Taking action also involves overcoming obstacles and challenges. It is essential to develop resilience and a growth mindset. Embrace failure as a learning opportunity and view setbacks as stepping stones towards success. Remember that every obstacle you encounter is an opportunity for growth and self-improvement.

Another crucial aspect of taking action is cultivating healthy habits. Identify habits that support your goals and well-being. This could include practicing mindfulness, exercising regularly, maintaining a healthy diet, or engaging in activities that bring you joy. By incorporating these habits into your daily routine, you create a foundation for personal growth and fulfillment.

Accountability and support are also essential when taking action towards fulfillment. Find a mentor, coach, or support group that can provide guidance, encouragement, and accountability. Surround yourself with positive influences who believe in your potential and can help you stay motivated during challenging times.

Taking action towards fulfillment requires consistency and perseverance. Recognize that self-discovery and empowerment are lifelong journeys, and progress may not always be linear. Celebrate your achievements, no matter how small, and be kind to yourself during moments of self-doubt.

In conclusion, taking action towards fulfillment is a crucial step in unlocking your true self. Set goals, break them down into manageable steps, overcome obstacles, cultivate healthy habits, seek support, and embrace a growth mindset. By actively participating in your own journey, you pave the way for self-discovery, personal growth, and a more fulfilling life.

Chapter 6: Overcoming Obstacles and Adversity

Developing Resilience and Perseverance

Resilience and perseverance are essential qualities for navigating the challenges and uncertainties of life. In this subchapter, we will explore practical strategies and insights to help you develop and strengthen these qualities within yourself.

Resilience is the ability to bounce back from adversity and to adapt to change. It is not about being immune to stress or difficulties but rather about how we respond to them. Resilient individuals have a growth mindset and see setbacks as opportunities for growth and learning. They possess a deep sense of self-belief and an unwavering determination to overcome obstacles.

One way to develop resilience is by cultivating a positive mindset. Focus on your strengths and achievements, and practice gratitude for the things you have. Surround yourself with positive influences and seek support from friends, family, or mentors who uplift and encourage you.

Another important aspect of resilience is self-care. Take care of your physical, mental, and emotional well-being. Engage in activities that bring you joy and relaxation, and make time for self-reflection and introspection. Develop healthy coping mechanisms, such as exercise, mindfulness, or journaling, to manage stress and build emotional resilience.

Perseverance, on the other hand, is the ability to persist in the face of challenges and setbacks. It requires determination, patience, and a strong sense of purpose. Persevering individuals understand that success often comes through hard work and perseverance, even when the path is difficult.

To develop perseverance, set clear goals for yourself and break them down into smaller, manageable steps. Celebrate small victories along the way to maintain motivation and momentum. Remember that setbacks are a part of the journey, and use them as opportunities for learning and growth. Develop a support system of like-minded individuals who can provide encouragement and accountability.

Developing resilience and perseverance is an ongoing process that requires commitment and practice. It is important to remember that everyone's journey is unique, and it is okay to make mistakes or experience setbacks. Embrace these challenges as opportunities for growth and continue to cultivate resilience and perseverance within yourself.

By developing these qualities, you will be better equipped to face the ups and downs of life with confidence and grace. Remember, you have the power to unlock your true self and create a life filled with resilience, perseverance, and personal growth.

Managing Stress and Anxiety

In today's fast-paced and demanding world, it is not uncommon for individuals, both young and old, to experience stress and anxiety. The pressures of school, relationships, and societal expectations can often feel overwhelming, leaving us feeling helpless and unsure of how to cope. However, by learning effective strategies for managing stress and anxiety, we can unlock our true selves and cultivate a sense of empowerment.

One of the first steps in managing stress and anxiety is to recognize and acknowledge our emotions. It is essential to understand that experiencing stress and anxiety is a normal part of life, and it does not define who we are as individuals. By accepting our emotions, we can begin to develop a healthy relationship with them and learn to navigate through challenging situations.

Next, it is crucial to establish a self-care routine. Self-care involves prioritizing our physical, mental, and emotional well-being. This can include activities such as exercise, meditation, journaling, or engaging in hobbies that bring us joy and relaxation. By taking care of ourselves, we can replenish our energy and build resilience to better handle stress and anxiety.

Additionally, developing healthy coping mechanisms is essential in managing stress and anxiety. This can involve practicing deep breathing exercises or engaging in mindfulness techniques to calm our minds and bodies. It is also beneficial to identify and challenge negative thoughts and replace them with positive affirmations. By reframing our thoughts, we can shift our perspective and approach stressful situations with a more positive mindset.

Furthermore, seeking support from trusted individuals is crucial in managing stress and anxiety. Whether it is talking to a friend, family member, or seeking professional help, sharing our feelings and concerns can provide valuable insight and guidance. It is important to remember that we are not alone in our struggles and that reaching out for support is a sign of strength, not weakness.

Finally, practicing patience and self-compassion is key in managing stress and anxiety. It is essential to recognize that progress takes time and setbacks are a normal part of the journey. By being kind and forgiving towards ourselves, we can cultivate a sense of resilience and continue moving forward towards self-discovery and empowerment.

In conclusion, managing stress and anxiety is an essential aspect of unlocking our true selves and cultivating empowerment. By recognizing and acknowledging our emotions, establishing a self-care routine, developing healthy coping mechanisms, seeking support, and practicing patience and self-compassion, we can navigate through life's challenges with resilience and discover our true potential. Remember, you have the power within you to overcome stress and anxiety and embrace a life of self-discovery and empowerment.

Coping with Failure and Rejection

Failure and rejection are inevitable parts of life that we all face at some point. Whether it's failing a test, not getting the job you wanted, or experiencing rejection in relationships, it can be incredibly challenging to deal with these setbacks. However, learning how to cope with failure and rejection is an essential skill that can lead to personal growth and empowerment.

First and foremost, it's crucial to remember that failure and rejection do not define your worth as a person. It's easy to let these experiences make you feel inadequate or like a failure, but that is far from the truth. Understanding that failure is a natural part of the learning process and that rejection often stems from external factors beyond your control can help you maintain a healthy perspective.

One effective way to cope with failure and rejection is to practice self-compassion. Treat yourself with kindness and understanding, just as you would a close friend. Acknowledge your emotions and allow yourself to feel disappointed or upset, but avoid dwelling on negative thoughts. Instead, focus on learning from the experience and using it as an opportunity for growth.

Another helpful strategy is to reframe your mindset. Instead of viewing failure and rejection as personal failures, see them as stepping stones toward success. Each setback is an opportunity to learn, adapt, and improve. Embrace a growth mindset, understanding that failure is not an endpoint but rather a part of the journey to success.

Seeking support is also crucial when coping with failure and rejection. Talk to trusted friends, family members, or mentors who can provide guidance and encouragement. Surrounding yourself with a strong support system can help you stay motivated and bounce back stronger than ever.

Lastly, it's essential to remember that failure and rejection are not permanent. They are temporary setbacks that can lead to future success if you maintain a positive attitude and persevere. Embrace resilience and keep pushing forward, even in the face of adversity.

In conclusion, coping with failure and rejection is a vital aspect of self-discovery and empowerment. By practicing self-compassion, reframing your mindset, seeking support, and maintaining resilience, you can navigate these challenges with grace and emerge stronger than ever. Remember, failure and rejection do not define you. They are merely opportunities for growth and learning on the path to unlocking your true self.

Seeking Support and Building a Supportive Network

In our journey of self-discovery and empowerment, it is important to recognize the value of seeking support and building a supportive network. No matter how strong and independent we may feel, we all need a helping hand and a shoulder to lean on at times. This subchapter explores the significance of seeking support and provides guidance on how to build a supportive network.

When we face challenges or difficult situations, it is natural to feel overwhelmed or anxious. However, bottling up our emotions and trying to handle everything on our own can be detrimental to our mental and emotional well-being. Seeking support allows us to share our burdens and gain different perspectives, ultimately helping us find solutions or cope with our struggles more effectively.

One way to seek support is by reaching out to trusted friends or family members. These individuals can provide a listening ear, offer comfort, and offer valuable advice based on their own experiences. It is important to remember that seeking support is not a sign of weakness but rather a sign of strength and self-awareness.

In addition to seeking support from those closest to us, it is also beneficial to build a supportive network outside of our immediate circle. This can be achieved through joining support groups, clubs, or organizations that align with our interests or goals. Surrounding ourselves with like-minded individuals who share similar struggles or aspirations can create a sense of belonging and provide a safe space for personal growth.

Furthermore, seeking professional support from therapists or counselors can be immensely helpful. These professionals are trained to guide us through our journey of self-discovery and provide valuable insights and tools for personal development. They can help us uncover the root causes of our anxieties, heal emotional wounds, and empower us to make positive changes in our lives.

Remember, building a supportive network is a two-way street. Just as we seek support, we must also be willing to offer support to others when needed. By being there for others, we not only strengthen our relationships but also gain a sense of fulfillment and purpose.

In conclusion, seeking support and building a supportive network are crucial aspects of our journey towards self-discovery and empowerment. By reaching out to others, we open ourselves up to new perspectives, gain valuable insights, and find comfort in knowing that we are not alone in our struggles. Whether it is seeking support from friends, family, professionals, or joining supportive communities, we are taking a proactive step towards unlocking our true selves and living a fulfilling life.

Chapter 7: Cultivating Healthy Relationships

Understanding the Importance of Healthy Relationships

In our journey of self-discovery and empowerment, one aspect that often gets overlooked is the significance of healthy relationships. As teens and adults, our lives are intertwined with others, and the quality of our relationships can greatly impact our overall well-being. In this subchapter, we will delve into the importance of nurturing healthy connections and how they contribute to our personal growth and happiness.

First and foremost, healthy relationships provide us with a sense of belonging and support. When we surround ourselves with individuals who genuinely care about our well-being, we feel valued and understood. These relationships serve as a safe space where we can share our joys, fears, and vulnerabilities without fear of judgment. The support we receive from these connections helps us navigate life's challenges and strengthens our resilience.

Furthermore, healthy relationships foster personal growth and self-awareness. Interacting with others allows us to learn from different perspectives and broaden our horizons. Through these connections, we gain insights into our own strengths and weaknesses, enabling us to work on areas that need improvement. Healthy relationships also provide accountability, motivating us to set and achieve personal goals.

Another crucial aspect of healthy relationships is the emotional and mental well-being they promote. Positive connections bring joy, happiness, and a sense of purpose into our lives. They provide a source of comfort and stability during difficult times, reducing stress and anxiety. Research has shown that individuals with strong relationships are generally happier and healthier, both mentally and physically.

Moreover, healthy relationships contribute to our overall self-esteem and self-worth. When we surround ourselves with people who uplift and support us, we feel more confident in ourselves and our abilities.

These connections remind us of our intrinsic value and help us develop a positive self-image.

In conclusion, understanding the importance of healthy relationships is vital for our self-discovery and empowerment. Nurturing positive connections provides us with a sense of belonging, support, and personal growth. They contribute to our emotional well-being, self-esteem, and overall happiness. By investing time and effort into fostering healthy relationships, we create a solid foundation for our journey of self-discovery and empowerment.

Enhancing Communication Skills

Effective communication skills are essential for building healthy relationships, expressing oneself clearly, and achieving personal and professional success. In this subchapter, we will explore various strategies and techniques to enhance your communication skills, allowing you to unlock your true self and empower yourself in your journey of self-discovery and personal growth.

1. Active Listening: One of the most important aspects of communication is listening actively. Practice giving your full attention to the speaker, maintaining eye contact, and avoiding distractions. This will not only improve your understanding but also foster trust and connection with others.

2. Non-Verbal Communication: Communication is not only about words; it also involves non-verbal cues such as body language, facial expressions, and gestures. Pay attention to your own non-verbal signals and learn to interpret them in others, as they can often convey emotions and intentions more accurately than words alone.

3. Empathy and Understanding: Developing empathy allows you to connect deeply with others and understand their emotions and perspectives. By putting yourself in someone else's shoes, you can create a safe and supportive environment for open and honest communication.

4. Effective Expression: Expressing yourself clearly and assertively is crucial in getting your message across. Practice using "I" statements to express your feelings and needs without blaming or criticizing others. This approach fosters open dialogue and promotes understanding.

5. Conflict Resolution: Conflict is a natural part of any relationship, but learning how to resolve conflicts peacefully is essential. Explore techniques such as active listening, compromise, and finding common ground to address and resolve conflicts effectively.

6. Mindful Communication: Mindfulness involves being fully present in the moment and aware of your thoughts, feelings, and actions. By practicing mindful communication, you can avoid misunderstandings, reduce stress, and build stronger connections with others.

7. Feedback and Reflection: Give and receive feedback constructively. Reflect on your own communication patterns and identify areas for improvement. Regular self-reflection can help you become more aware of your communication style and make necessary adjustments.

Remember, enhancing communication skills is an ongoing process. Practice these techniques consistently, and you will gradually develop stronger connections and improve your overall communication effectiveness. By unlocking your true self through effective communication, you will empower yourself to navigate life's challenges with confidence and create meaningful relationships that contribute to your personal growth and well-being.

Setting Boundaries and Respecting Others' Boundaries

In the journey of self-discovery and empowerment, one crucial aspect that often gets overlooked is the importance of setting boundaries and respecting the boundaries of others. Boundaries play a fundamental role in establishing healthy relationships, fostering personal growth, and protecting our mental and emotional well-being. This subchapter will delve into the significance of setting boundaries, understanding the different types of boundaries, and provide practical tips for respecting the boundaries of others.

Setting boundaries is all about understanding and communicating our limits. It involves recognizing what makes us feel comfortable or uncomfortable and expressing these limits to others in a respectful manner. By setting boundaries, we create a safe space for ourselves where we can thrive and grow without unnecessary stress or pressure. It is a way of asserting our needs and values, maintaining self-respect, and ensuring that our relationships are built on mutual understanding and respect.

There are various types of boundaries that we should be aware of. Physical boundaries involve personal space and touch, emotional boundaries encompass our feelings and vulnerabilities, and intellectual boundaries relate to our thoughts and beliefs. By understanding these different types of boundaries, we can identify the areas where we may need to set limits and protect ourselves from potential harm or discomfort.

Respecting the boundaries of others is equally important. Just as we have the right to set boundaries, we must also respect the boundaries of those around us. This involves actively listening to others, acknowledging their limits, and refraining from crossing those boundaries. Respecting others' boundaries nurtures trust, empathy, and healthy communication within relationships.

To effectively navigate the realm of boundaries, it is essential to practice self-awareness and open communication. Reflect on your personal needs and values, and be honest with yourself about what feels right and what doesn't. Communicate your boundaries clearly, using "I" statements to express your feelings and needs without blaming or criticizing others. Similarly, when interacting with others, be attentive to their verbal and non-verbal cues, and be mindful of their boundaries.

Remember, setting and respecting boundaries is an ongoing process that requires practice and self-reflection. It is not about building walls or shutting others out; rather, it is about cultivating healthy, balanced relationships and fostering personal growth. By embracing boundaries, you unlock the power to protect your well-being, make informed choices, and build meaningful connections with others.

Navigating Conflict and Resolving Issues

Conflict is an inevitable part of life. Whether it arises in our personal relationships, at school, or in the workplace, conflicts can be challenging and overwhelming. However, understanding how to navigate conflicts and effectively resolve issues is crucial for personal growth and empowerment. In this subchapter, we will explore strategies and techniques that will help you unlock your true self and navigate conflict with confidence.

1. Understanding the nature of conflict: Conflict arises from differences in opinions, values, or needs. It is important to recognize that conflict is not inherently negative; it can be an opportunity for growth and understanding.

2. Practicing effective communication: Clear and open communication is vital in resolving conflicts. By actively listening and expressing your thoughts and feelings assertively, you can foster understanding and find common ground.

3. Developing empathy and perspective-taking: Empathy allows us to understand and appreciate the feelings and perspectives of others. By putting ourselves in someone else's shoes, we can foster compassion and find collaborative solutions.

4. Recognizing your triggers and emotions: Conflict often triggers emotional responses. By becoming aware of your triggers, you can manage your emotions effectively and respond rather than react impulsively.

5. Finding common ground: Focus on areas of agreement rather than differences. Identifying shared goals or interests can help build bridges and facilitate resolution.

6. Seeking compromise and negotiation: In many conflicts, a win-win solution is possible through compromise and negotiation. Be willing to explore alternative options and find mutually beneficial agreements.

7. Seeking support and mediation when needed: Sometimes, conflicts can be complex or emotionally charged. In such cases, seeking the help of a trusted adult, mentor, or professional mediator can provide valuable guidance and support.

8. Learning from conflicts: Every conflict offers an opportunity for learning and personal growth. Reflect on the conflict and identify lessons learned, as well as areas for self-improvement.

9. Practicing self-care: Conflict can be emotionally draining. Engaging in self-care activities such as exercise, mindfulness, and hobbies can help you manage stress and maintain your well-being during challenging times.

By mastering the art of navigating conflict and resolving issues, you can unlock your true self and empower yourself to overcome challenges. Remember, conflict is a natural part of life, but with the right tools and mindset, you can transform conflicts into opportunities for growth and positive change.

Chapter 8: Embracing Self-Expression and Authenticity

Discovering and Honoring Your True Self

Subchapter: Discovering and Honoring Your True Self

Introduction: In this subchapter, we will delve into the transformative journey of self-discovery and empowerment. Understanding and honoring your true self is the key to unlocking a fulfilling and purposeful life. Through self-reflection, awareness, and healing, you can overcome anxiety and embark on a path of self-help and personal growth. Whether you are a teen or an adult, this chapter will provide you with valuable insights and actionable steps towards discovering your authentic self.

Understanding the Concept of True Self: The concept of the true self refers to the essence of who you are, beyond the societal expectations and external influences. It is about recognizing your values, passions, strengths, and unique qualities that make you who you are. Discovering your true self is a continuous journey of self-reflection and self-awareness.

The Importance of Self-Reflection: Self-reflection is a powerful tool for self-discovery. It allows you to go inward and examine your thoughts, emotions, and behaviors. By asking yourself thought-provoking questions, you can gain a deeper understanding of your desires, fears, and aspirations. The 300 questions provided in this book will serve as a guide to assist you in this introspective process.

Uncovering Your Passions and Purpose: Identifying your passions is a crucial step in honoring your true self. Explore different activities, hobbies, and interests that bring you joy and fulfillment. Pay attention to the activities that make you lose track of time and evoke a sense of flow. These are often indicators of your true passions and can lead you towards your life's purpose.

Embracing Your Authenticity: In a world that often pressures us to conform, embracing your authenticity is a radical act of self-empowerment. It involves accepting and loving yourself unconditionally, flaws and all. Celebrate your uniqueness and cultivate self-compassion. By being true to yourself, you inspire others to do the same.

Healing and Overcoming Anxiety: Self-discovery and empowerment go hand in hand with healing. Addressing past traumas, limiting beliefs, and negative thought patterns is essential for unleashing your true potential. This chapter will provide you with techniques and strategies to overcome anxiety, promote self-healing, and foster a positive mindset.

Conclusion: Discovering and honoring your true self is a lifelong journey that requires patience, self-compassion, and a commitment to growth. By engaging in self-reflection, embracing authenticity, and healing past wounds, you will unlock the door to self-discovery and empowerment. This subchapter will equip you with the necessary tools to embark on this transformative journey towards self-help and personal growth.

Expressing Yourself Creatively

Creativity is a powerful tool for self-expression and personal growth. In this subchapter, we will explore various ways in which you can tap into your creative side to unlock your true self. Whether you consider yourself an artist or not, expressing yourself creatively can be an incredibly fulfilling and therapeutic experience.

One of the most accessible ways to express yourself creatively is through journaling or writing. By putting your thoughts and emotions on paper, you give them a voice and a tangible form. This can help you gain clarity, release pent-up feelings, and develop a deeper understanding of yourself. Try free-writing or exploring different writing prompts to get your creative juices flowing.

If you enjoy visual arts, consider exploring different mediums such as painting, drawing, or photography. Engaging in these activities allows you to express your emotions and experiences visually. Don't worry about creating a masterpiece; focus on the process and the joy of creating. Experiment with colors, textures, and techniques to find what resonates with you.

Music can also be a powerful outlet for self-expression. Whether you play an instrument, sing, or simply enjoy listening, music has the ability to evoke emotions and convey messages that words alone cannot. Consider learning to play an instrument, joining a choir or band, or simply creating playlists that reflect your mood or current state of mind.

Another form of creative expression is through movement. Dance, yoga, or any form of physical activity can help you connect with your body and express yourself in a nonverbal way. Explore different styles and find what brings you joy and a sense of liberation. You don't need to be a professional dancer; the purpose is to let go, move freely, and express yourself authentically.

Lastly, don't be afraid to explore unconventional forms of creativity. Cooking, gardening, crafting, or even building with Legos can all be avenues for self-expression. The key is to engage in activities that allow you to tap into your imagination, explore your emotions, and express yourself authentically.

Remember, the goal of expressing yourself creatively is not to achieve perfection or create something for others to admire. It is about finding joy, release, and a deeper connection with yourself. So, embrace your unique creative spirit and let it guide you on your journey of self-discovery and empowerment.

Embracing Your Unique Qualities and Individuality

In a world that often tries to fit us into molds and conform to societal norms, it can be challenging to embrace our unique qualities and individuality. However, it is essential for our self-discovery, personal growth, and overall well-being. This subchapter will delve into the importance of embracing your uniqueness and provide practical tips on how to do so.

Firstly, it is crucial to understand that each one of us possesses a set of qualities and traits that make us unique. These qualities can range from our physical appearance, talents, skills, personality traits, and even our life experiences. Recognizing and appreciating these qualities is the first step towards embracing your individuality.

One of the keys to embracing your uniqueness is self-acceptance. It involves acknowledging and embracing all aspects of yourself, including the ones you might perceive as flaws or weaknesses. By accepting yourself wholly, you can let go of self-judgment and comparison to others, freeing yourself to explore your true potential.

Another important aspect is self-expression. Embracing your individuality means allowing yourself to express who you truly are, without fearing judgment or rejection. Whether it is through art, writing, music, or any other form of creative outlet, find ways to express your thoughts, feelings, and ideas authentically. This will not only help you discover more about yourself but also inspire others to do the same.

Moreover, surround yourself with a supportive and accepting community. Seek out individuals who celebrate diversity and encourage personal growth. Engaging with like-minded people who appreciate and value your uniqueness can provide a sense of belonging and empowerment.

Lastly, understanding that embracing your individuality is a lifelong journey is crucial. As you grow and evolve, your unique qualities may change and develop. Embrace the process of self-discovery and be open to exploring new aspects of your individuality.

In conclusion, embracing your unique qualities and individuality is fundamental to your self-discovery and empowerment. By practicing self-acceptance, expressing yourself authentically, finding a supportive community, and embracing the ongoing journey of self-discovery, you will unlock your true self and live a fulfilling life that aligns with your values and passions. Remember, you are unique, and that uniqueness is what makes you truly extraordinary.

Building Confidence and Assertiveness

Confidence and assertiveness are two essential traits that can greatly impact our lives, shaping the way we interact with others and the world around us. In this subchapter, we will explore practical strategies and techniques to help you build and enhance your confidence and assertiveness, empowering you to unlock your true self.

1. Understanding Confidence: Confidence is not something we are born with; it is a skill that can be developed and strengthened over time. We will delve into the concept of self-esteem and self-worth, helping you recognize your unique qualities and strengths. Through self-reflection and self-awareness exercises, you will gain a deeper understanding of your true value and potential.

2. Embracing Self-Compassion: Developing confidence requires practicing self-compassion. We will guide you through exercises that encourage self-acceptance, forgiveness, and love. By treating yourself with kindness and understanding, you will build a solid foundation for your self-confidence journey.

3. Overcoming Fear and Self-Doubt: Fear and self-doubt often hold us back from reaching our full potential. We will explore various strategies to help you overcome these limiting beliefs, replacing them with positive affirmations and empowering thoughts. Through a series of reflective questions, you will learn to challenge and reframe negative self-talk, boosting your self-confidence.

4. Developing Assertiveness Skills: Assertiveness is the ability to express ourselves effectively and stand up for our rights while respecting others. We will provide practical tips and techniques to help you develop assertiveness skills, such as effective communication, setting boundaries, and saying no when necessary. Through role-playing exercises and real-life scenarios, you will gain the confidence to assert yourself in various situations.

5. Building Resilience: Building confidence and assertiveness requires resilience, as setbacks and challenges are inevitable. We will guide you through resilience-building exercises, helping you develop a positive mindset, adapt to change, and bounce back from failures. By embracing challenges as opportunities for growth, you will strengthen your confidence and assertiveness.

Building confidence and assertiveness is an ongoing journey, and it requires consistent practice and self-reflection. Throughout this subchapter, you will find a range of self-help exercises, reflection questions, and practical tips to support your personal growth. By cultivating these essential traits, you will unlock your true self, empowering yourself to navigate life with confidence and assertiveness. Remember, you have the power to shape your own destiny and become the best version of yourself.

Chapter 9: Igniting Personal Growth and Transformation

Continual Learning and Personal Development

In our journey of self-discovery and empowerment, one of the key elements that play a vital role is continual learning and personal development. The process of growth and self-improvement is an ongoing journey that helps us unlock our true potential and become the best version of ourselves.

Continual learning refers to the practice of acquiring new knowledge, skills, and experiences throughout our lives. It is about embracing curiosity, being open to new ideas, and seeking opportunities for growth. By actively engaging in learning, we broaden our horizons, expand our perspectives, and challenge our existing beliefs and limitations.

Personal development, on the other hand, focuses on enhancing our self-awareness, emotional intelligence, and overall well-being. It involves the conscious effort to develop and improve various aspects of our lives, including our relationships, career, health, and mindset. By investing in personal development, we can cultivate a sense of purpose, boost our self-confidence, and lead a more fulfilling life.

For teenagers and adults alike, the journey of self-help and personal growth can be transformative. It allows us to discover our passions, strengths, and values, and align them with our goals and aspirations. Moreover, it equips us with the necessary tools and strategies to navigate life's challenges, manage stress, and cultivate resilience.

Self-help resources such as "Unlocking Your True Self: A Teen's Guide to Self-Discovery and Empowerment" provide a roadmap for individuals seeking personal development. Through self-reflection, awareness, and healing exercises, readers can embark on a journey of self-discovery and empowerment.

By incorporating the principles of continual learning and personal development into our lives, we can foster a growth mindset and embrace lifelong learning. We can actively seek out opportunities for growth, whether it be through reading books, attending workshops, or engaging in meaningful conversations with others.

As we continue our journey of self-help and personal growth, it is important to remember that it is not a destination but a lifelong process. We must be patient with ourselves, celebrate our progress, and remain open to new possibilities. By investing in our personal development, we can unlock our true potential, live a more authentic life, and inspire others to do the same.

Embracing Change and Adaptability

Change is an inevitable part of life. It can be exciting, terrifying, and everything in between. As a teenager, you are in a unique phase of life where change is happening rapidly and consistently. From physical and emotional changes to shifts in your relationships and responsibilities, adapting to change is crucial for your personal growth and empowerment.

In this subchapter, we will explore the concept of embracing change and developing adaptability as essential skills for navigating through life's challenges and uncertainties. By understanding and harnessing the power of change, you can unlock your true self and embark on a journey of self-discovery and empowerment.

Change provides us with opportunities for growth and self-improvement. It pushes us out of our comfort zones and forces us to confront new experiences, ideas, and perspectives. Embracing change means accepting that it is a natural and necessary part of life, and that resisting it only hinders our progress.

Adaptability, on the other hand, refers to our ability to adjust and thrive in the face of change. It involves being flexible, open-minded, and resilient. Developing adaptability allows us to navigate through life's twists and turns with grace and confidence.

In this subchapter, we will explore various strategies and techniques to help you embrace change and cultivate adaptability. We will discuss the importance of self-reflection and awareness in understanding how change affects you personally. Through a series of thought-provoking questions and exercises, you will be encouraged to examine your fears, beliefs, and attitudes towards change.

Additionally, we will delve into practical tools and practices that can aid in building adaptability. From cultivating a growth mindset and practicing mindfulness to seeking support from others and developing a sense of purpose, these strategies will equip you with the skills needed to thrive in an ever-changing world.

Remember, change is not something to be feared or avoided. It is an opportunity for growth, self-discovery, and empowerment. By embracing change and developing adaptability, you can unlock your true self and embark on a transformative journey towards a fulfilling and empowered life.

Are you ready to take the first step towards embracing change and cultivating adaptability? Let's embark on this journey together and unlock your true potential.

Taking Risks and Stepping Out of Your Comfort Zone

In the journey of self-discovery and empowerment, one crucial aspect that often gets overlooked is the willingness to take risks and step out of our comfort zones. It is natural for humans to seek comfort and security, but true growth and transformation lie in embracing the unknown and challenging ourselves in new ways. This subchapter aims to shed light on the significance of taking risks and provide guidance on how to do so effectively.

Taking risks is essential for personal development as it allows us to break free from the limitations we set for ourselves. By stepping out of our comfort zones, we open ourselves up to new experiences, opportunities, and perspectives. It is through these experiences that we truly discover who we are and what we are capable of achieving.

One of the first steps towards taking risks is identifying our fears and understanding what holds us back. Fear often stems from uncertainty or the fear of failure. However, it is important to realize that failure is a part of growth and should be embraced as a learning opportunity. By reframing failure as an essential stepping stone towards success, we can overcome our fears and take calculated risks.

To effectively step out of our comfort zones, it is crucial to set clear goals and create a plan of action. Start by identifying areas in your life where you feel stagnant or unfulfilled. Whether it is trying a new hobby, pursuing a different career path, or expressing yourself creatively, take small steps towards those goals. Break them down into manageable tasks and celebrate each milestone along the way. Remember, progress is more important than perfection.

Surrounding yourself with a supportive network can also greatly impact your ability to take risks. Seek out mentors, friends, or family members who encourage and uplift you. Their guidance and perspective can provide the necessary motivation and reassurance when faced with uncertainty.

In conclusion, taking risks and stepping out of your comfort zone is an integral part of self-discovery and empowerment. By embracing the unknown, challenging our fears, and setting clear goals, we can unlock our true potential and create a life that aligns with our authentic selves. Remember, the magic happens outside of our comfort zones, and it is through taking risks that we truly find ourselves. So, dare to dream, dare to take action, and dare to step into the unknown. The world is waiting for you to step up and unlock your true self.

Celebrating Your Growth and Progress

In the journey of self-discovery and empowerment, it is crucial to acknowledge and celebrate your growth and progress. This subchapter aims to remind you of the importance of recognizing your achievements and milestones, and how it can contribute to your overall well-being and personal development.

Often, we get caught up in the pursuit of our goals and dreams that we forget to appreciate the small victories along the way. Celebrating your growth and progress not only boosts your self-esteem but also provides motivation to keep pushing forward. It serves as a reminder that you are capable of overcoming challenges and that your efforts are paying off.

One powerful way to celebrate your growth is by reflecting on your journey. Take a moment to look back at where you started and how far you have come. Ask yourself the following questions: What were the obstacles you faced? How did you overcome them? What lessons did you learn? By acknowledging the progress you have made, you gain a deeper understanding of your own resilience and strength.

Another way to celebrate your growth is by setting milestones and rewarding yourself when you achieve them. These milestones can be both big and small, and should align with your personal goals. Treat yourself to something you enjoy, such as a day off, a favorite meal, or a new book. This not only gives you a sense of accomplishment but also creates positive associations with your progress.

In addition to personal celebrations, it is also important to share your achievements with others. Surround yourself with a supportive community that recognizes and celebrates your growth. Whether it is friends, family, or mentors, sharing your accomplishments allows you to feel validated and encouraged. Moreover, it inspires others to pursue their own growth and progress.

Remember, celebrating your growth and progress is not about bragging or seeking validation from others. It is about recognizing your own worth and the efforts you have put into becoming the best version of yourself. Embrace each milestone as a stepping stone towards your personal growth and use it as fuel to continue your journey of self-discovery and empowerment.

By celebrating your growth and progress, you cultivate a positive mindset, build self-confidence, and stay motivated on your path to unlocking your true self. Embrace the journey and take pride in the progress you make, for every step forward is a testament to your growth and resilience.

Chapter 10: Sustaining Your True Self

Building Habits for Sustainable Self-Discovery

In our journey of self-discovery and personal growth, it is essential to develop habits that support sustainable progress. Building habits that promote self-awareness, healing, and empowerment can transform our lives and help us navigate the challenges of teenage years and adulthood. This subchapter aims to provide insights and practical advice on how to cultivate these habits effectively.

1. Daily Reflection: Start by setting aside a few minutes each day for self-reflection. Ask yourself questions from the book "300 Questions for Self-Reflection, Awareness, Discovery, Healing, and Anti-anxiety." This exercise will help you gain clarity about your emotions, thoughts, and aspirations.

2. Mindfulness Practice: Incorporate mindfulness into your daily routine. Engage in activities such as meditation, deep breathing exercises, or mindful walks. These practices enable you to stay present in the moment and develop a deeper understanding of yourself.

3. Journaling: Maintain a journal to express your thoughts, emotions, and experiences. This habit allows you to reflect on your progress, identify patterns, and gain valuable insights into your true self.

4. Healthy Lifestyle: Nurture your mind and body by adopting a healthy lifestyle. Ensure you get sufficient sleep, eat nutritious meals, and engage in regular physical activity. Taking care of your physical well-being contributes to mental clarity and overall self-discovery.

5. Surround Yourself with Positive Influences: Evaluate the people and environments you surround yourself with. Seek out individuals who inspire and support your growth. Engage in activities and surround yourself with environments that align with your values and aspirations.

6. Seek Knowledge: Continuously seek knowledge and expand your horizons. Read books, attend workshops, listen to podcasts, or engage in online courses that foster self-discovery and personal

growth. This habit will help you develop a broader perspective and gain new insights into yourself and the world around you.

7. Embrace Vulnerability: Embracing vulnerability is crucial for self-discovery. Allow yourself to be open and authentic, both with yourself and others. Embracing vulnerability can lead to deeper connections, self-acceptance, and personal growth.

8. Practice Self-Compassion: Be kind to yourself throughout your journey. Understand that self-discovery is a process, and it's okay to make mistakes and face setbacks. Practice self-compassion by treating yourself with kindness, understanding, and forgiveness.

By incorporating these habits into your daily life, you can cultivate sustainable self-discovery and personal growth. Remember, these habits take time to develop and integrate into your routine, so be patient with yourself. Unlocking your true self is a lifelong journey, and with consistent effort and dedication, you can empower yourself to live a fulfilling and authentic life.

Creating a Supportive Environment

In the journey of self-discovery and empowerment, one crucial aspect that often goes overlooked is the importance of creating a supportive environment. As teenagers and adults, we must recognize that our surroundings play a significant role in shaping our thoughts, emotions, and overall well-being. By consciously curating a supportive environment, we can enhance our self-help endeavors and pave the way for personal growth and healing.

The first step towards creating a supportive environment is identifying the elements that contribute positively to our mental and emotional health. Take a moment to reflect on the people, places, and activities that uplift and inspire you. Surrounding yourself with individuals who believe in your potential and encourage your growth is essential. Seek out friends, mentors, or support groups that share your interests and values, and who genuinely want to see you succeed. Engaging in activities that align with your passions can also bring a sense of fulfillment and motivation.

Another crucial aspect of a supportive environment is a physical space that nurtures your well-being. Designate a peaceful corner in your room or create a cozy reading nook where you can unwind and reflect. Decorate your space with items that inspire and motivate you, such as meaningful quotes, artwork, or photographs. A clutter-free environment can promote a sense of calm and clarity, allowing for more effective self-reflection and self-help practices.

Additionally, it is vital to cultivate a supportive internal dialogue. Negative self-talk can hinder our progress and erode our self-esteem. Practice self-compassion and challenge negative thoughts with positive affirmations. Surround yourself with literature, podcasts, or online communities that promote self-help, personal growth, and empowerment. Engaging with these resources can provide guidance, validation, and a sense of belonging.

Remember, creating a supportive environment is an ongoing process that requires consistent effort and evaluation. Regularly assess your surroundings and relationships to ensure they align with your goals and values. Be open to making necessary changes, even if it means letting go of people or situations that no longer serve your growth.

By investing in a supportive environment, you are creating a solid foundation for your self-help journey. Embrace the power of your surroundings and take control of your growth and healing. Unlock your true self by surrounding yourself with positivity, support, and inspiration.

Practicing Self-Reflection and Evaluation

In our journey towards self-discovery and empowerment, it is crucial to develop the habit of self-reflection and evaluation. This subchapter will delve into the importance of self-reflection, provide guidance on how to practice it effectively, and offer tools for evaluating our progress.

Self-reflection is the process of stepping back and objectively analyzing our thoughts, feelings, and actions. It allows us to gain a deeper understanding of ourselves, our motivations, and the impact we have on others. By taking the time to reflect, we can identify patterns, strengths, weaknesses, and areas for growth. It is a powerful tool for personal development and self-improvement.

To practice self-reflection effectively, it is essential to create a quiet and safe space for introspection. Find a comfortable place free from distractions, where you can focus solely on yourself. Begin by asking yourself open-ended questions such as, "What am I feeling right now?," "What challenges am I facing?," or "What are my goals and aspirations?" These questions will help you uncover your true thoughts and emotions.

The book "Unlocking Your True Self: A Teen's Guide to Self-Discovery and Empowerment" offers a comprehensive list of 300 questions specifically crafted for self-reflection, awareness, discovery, healing, and anti-anxiety. These questions are designed to spark introspection and encourage personal growth. They cover various aspects of life, including relationships, self-esteem, goals, fears, and dreams. Answering these questions honestly and thoughtfully will provide valuable insights into your inner world.

In addition to self-reflection, regular evaluation is necessary to track our progress and make necessary adjustments. Evaluation involves assessing our actions, behaviors, and choices to determine if they align with our values and goals. By evaluating our actions, we can identify areas where we may need to improve or change course. This practice ensures that we are continuously growing and evolving towards our true potential.

In conclusion, practicing self-reflection and evaluation is a vital part of our journey towards self-discovery and empowerment. By dedicating time to introspection, answering thought-provoking questions, and evaluating our progress, we can gain a deeper understanding of ourselves and make positive changes. The book "Unlocking Your True Self: A Teen's Guide to Self-Discovery and Empowerment" provides a valuable resource for teenagers and adults seeking self-help and personal growth. Embrace the power of self-reflection and evaluation, and unlock your true potential.

Embracing a Lifelong Journey of Self-Discovery

In a world filled with constant distractions and pressures, it is easy to lose sight of who we truly are. However, the path to self-discovery is an essential journey that we should all embark on. It is through self-discovery that we can find our true selves and unlock our full potential. In the subchapter titled "Embracing a Lifelong Journey of Self-Discovery," we will explore the importance of self-discovery, the benefits it brings, and practical steps to embark on this transformative journey.

Self-discovery is the process of getting to know oneself on a deeper level. It involves examining our thoughts, beliefs, values, and desires. By understanding ourselves better, we can make informed decisions, set meaningful goals, and lead a more authentic and fulfilling life. This journey is not a one-time event but rather a lifelong process. It requires us to continuously learn, grow, and evolve.

Embracing a lifelong journey of self-discovery brings numerous benefits. Firstly, it allows us to cultivate self-awareness. By understanding our strengths, weaknesses, and triggers, we can navigate life's challenges with greater ease and resilience. Self-discovery also empowers us to make choices aligned with our values and passions, leading to a sense of purpose and fulfillment. Furthermore, it enhances our relationships with others, as we develop a deeper understanding and empathy for their unique journeys.

To embark on this transformative journey, we can begin by asking ourselves thought-provoking questions. In the book "Unlocking Your True Self: A Teen's Guide to Self-Discovery and Empowerment," you will find a collection of 300 questions designed to facilitate self-reflection, awareness, and healing. These questions cover various aspects of life, such as personal values, goals, relationships, fears, and dreams. By taking the time to answer these questions honestly and introspectively, you will gain invaluable insights into your true self.

Additionally, the book offers practical techniques and exercises to aid in self-discovery. From journaling and meditation to creative expression and mindfulness, these tools provide avenues for self-exploration and growth. The book also encourages seeking support from trusted mentors, therapists, or support groups who can guide you on your journey.

In conclusion, embracing a lifelong journey of self-discovery is a powerful step towards personal growth and empowerment. By delving deep within ourselves, we can uncover our true passions, values, and dreams. "Unlocking Your True Self: A Teen's Guide to Self-Discovery and Empowerment" provides a roadmap for this transformative journey, offering a collection of questions and practical tools to aid in self-reflection and awareness. Embark on this journey, and you will unlock the door to a more authentic, fulfilling, and empowered life.

Conclusion: Embracing Your True Self and Empowering Others

In the journey of self-discovery and empowerment, the most important lesson to learn is to embrace your true self. Throughout this book, we have explored various aspects of self-reflection, awareness, and healing. Now, it is time to put all that knowledge into practice and unlock the true potential within you.

Embracing your true self begins with accepting who you are, both your strengths and weaknesses. It means acknowledging your passions, talents, and dreams, and aligning your actions with your authentic self. When you embrace your true self, you radiate confidence and authenticity, which inspires others to do the same.

Self-help is not just about improving yourself; it is also about empowering others. As you embark on your journey of self-discovery, remember to uplift and encourage those around you. By sharing your experiences, insights, and wisdom, you can help others find their own path to self-empowerment.

One way to empower others is by practicing active listening and empathy. Truly hearing someone's story and understanding their emotions creates a safe space for them to embrace their true selves. Offer support, encouragement, and guidance without judgment, allowing them to discover their own strengths and find their voice.

Another powerful way to empower others is by leading by example. When you embrace your true self, you become a role model for others to follow. Show them that life's challenges can be overcome, that self-love and acceptance are possible, and that dreams can be turned into reality. Your authenticity and courage will inspire them to do the same.

As you continue on your journey of self-discovery and empowerment, remember that it is a lifelong process. Embracing your true self is not a destination but a continuous evolution. Be open to change, embrace new experiences, and never stop learning.

In conclusion, unlocking your true self is a powerful and transformative journey. By embracing who you truly are, you not only find happiness and fulfillment within yourself but also empower those around you. Through self-reflection, awareness, and healing, you can overcome anxiety and discover the incredible potential that lies within you. Share your knowledge and experiences with others, and together, let us create a world where everyone is empowered to embrace their true selves and live their best lives.